OPPOSITES
All Around Me!

WET and
DRY

A Crabtree Roots Book

CRABTREE
Publishing Company
www.crabtreebooks.com

AMY CULLIFORD

School-to-Home Support for Caregivers and Teachers

This book helps children grow by letting them practice reading. Here are a few guiding questions to help the reader with building his or her comprehension skills. Possible answers appear here in red.

Before Reading:

• What do I think this book is about?
  - *This book is about wet things and dry things.*
  - *This book is about opposites.*

• What do I want to learn about this topic?
  - *I want to learn what wet things look like.*
  - *I want to learn what the opposite of dry is.*

During Reading:

• I wonder why...
  - *I wonder why streets get wet.*
  - *I wonder why things dry.*

• What have I learned so far?
  - *I have learned that streets can be wet and dry.*
  - *I have learned what wet looks like.*

After Reading:

• What details did I learn about this topic?
  - *I have learned that slides can be wet.*
  - *I have learned what dogs look like both wet and dry.*

• Read the book again and look for the vocabulary words.
  - *I see the word **street** on page 5 and the word **slide** on page 8. The other vocabulary words are found on page 14.*

What is **wet**, and
what is **dry**?

The **street** is wet.

The street is dry.

This **slide** is wet.

This slide is dry.

This **dog** is wet.

This dog is dry.

Word List

Sight Words

and	the	what
is	this	

Words to Know

dog

dry

slide

street

wet

31 Words

What is **wet**, and what is **dry**?

The **street** is wet.

The street is dry.

This **slide** is wet.

This slide is dry.

This **dog** is wet.

This dog is dry.

CRABTREE Publishing Company

Written by: Amy Culliford

Designed by: Rhea Wallace

Series Development: James Earley

Proofreader: Ellen Rodger

Educational Consultant: Marie Lemke M.Ed.

Photographs:
Shutterstock: photomaster: cover (left); TSEKhimster: cover (right); DenisNata: p. 1 (left); Lubava: p. 1 (right); Kaentian Street: p. 3, 14; Jayakrit Hirisajja: p. 4, 14; WeStudio: p. 7; Lee Waranyu: p. 8, 9, 14; Lunja: p. 11, 14; Reddogs: p. 12-13

OPPOSITES

All Around Me!

WET and DRY

Library and Archives Canada Cataloguing in Publication

Title: Wet and dry / Amy Culliford.
Names: Culliford, Amy, 1992- author.
 Description: Series statement: Opposites all around me! | "A Crabtree roots book".
Identifiers: Canadiana (print) 20210159359 | Canadiana (ebook) 20210159367 | ISBN 9781427140210
 (hardcover) | ISBN 9781427140272 (softcover) | ISBN 9781427133588 (HTML) | ISBN 9781427140333
 (read-along ebook) | ISBN 9781427134189 (EPUB)
Subjects: LCSH: Water—Juvenile literature. | LCSH: Polarity—Juvenile literature. | LCSH: English
 language—Synonyms and antonyms—Juvenile literature.
Classification: LCC QC920 .C85 2021 | DDC j546/.22—dc23

Library of Congress Cataloging-in-Publication Data

Names: Culliford, Amy, 1992- author.
Title: Wet and dry / Amy Culliford.
Description: New York, NY : Crabtree Publishing Company, [2022] | Series:
 Opposites all around me - a crabtree roots book | Includes index. |
 Audience: Ages 4-6 | Audience: Grades K-1
Identifiers: LCCN 2021010788 (print) | LCCN 2021010789 (ebook) | ISBN
 9781427140210 (hardcover) | ISBN 9781427140272 (paperback) | ISBN
 9781427133588 (ebook) | ISBN 9781427134189 (epub) | ISBN 9781427140333
 (read along)
Subjects: LCSH: Water--Juvenile literature. | Evaporation--Juvenile
 literature. | Polarity--Juvenile literature. | English
 language--Synonyms and antonyms--Juvenile literature.
Classification: LCC QC920 .C85 2022 (print) | LCC QC920 (ebook) | DDC
 553.7--dc23
LC record available at https://lccn.loc.gov/2021010788
LC ebook record available at https://lccn.loc.gov/2021010789

Crabtree Publishing Company

www.crabtreebooks.com   1-800-387-7650

Published in the United States
Crabtree Publishing
347 Fifth Avenue, Suite 1402-145
New York, NY, 10016

Published in Canada
Crabtree Publishing
616 Welland Ave.
St. Catharines, Ontario L2M 5V6